True-Crime Story

The Osage Murders and the Reign of Terror

ROBERT KENNEDY

Table of Contents

Introduction

In-depth history of the Osage Nation pre-oil discovery

The Osage are thought to have arisen as a separate people from among the Siouan speaking tribal groups who lived in the Ohio River valley region, which included modern-day Ohio, Indiana, Illinois, West Virginia, and Kentucky.

Archaeological evidence suggests that their ancestors lived in this region as early as 1000 AD.

Linguistic study links the Osage language to a shared ancestral Siouan tongue, with the Quapaw tribe being the closest cousins. Oral traditions provide accounts of ancestor migrations westward along the rivers.

By the late 1500s, Siouan tribes such as the Omaha, Ponca, and Osage had established themselves around the junction of the Missouri and Ohio rivers.

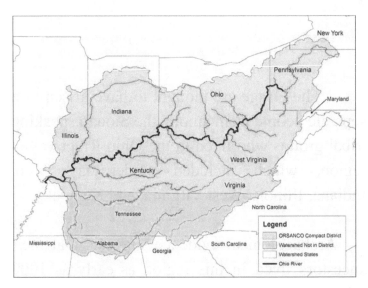

Map of osage

The proto-Osage formed with shared traditions of patrilineal clan systems, woodland horticulture, and seasonal bison hunting as these ancient tribes established separate cultural patterns over millennia.

The villages were made out of thatched wigwams organized in circular patterns around central plazas. Shamans were prominent religious figures, and rituals included ritualized dance.

Bows and arrows, stone-lined earth ovens, pottery, and wood/bone/antler implements all represented forest adaptations.

Bison and deer provided meat, skins, and bones, while women grew maize, beans, and squash. To exchange unusual items like shells and copper, trade networks stretched hundreds of kilometers.

Increased pressures from increasing Iroquois and Cherokee tribes presumably forced the proto-Osage westward by the late 1500s.

With a population of 10,000 people organized into autonomous communities under clan leadership, they settled in the lush river basins of the Osage, Gasconade, and Missouri Rivers.

Prior to European contact, the Osage Nation emerged with a separate culture and territory.

Proto-osage village

Many Osage people became terribly ill in the 1600s as a result of germs carried by European visitors.

Smallpox and other diseases spread quickly. Many Osage perished because their bodies were not used to these new illnesses.

Because there were fewer Osage around, other tribes began battling with them for territory and resources. Food, water, and places to live were scarce. The Cherokee and Sauk tribes were interested in the Osage territory.

It was more difficult to protect their land now that there were fewer Osage households.

Other groups, such as the Cherokee and Sauk, capitalized on this. They marched into Osage territory, capturing hunting grounds and communities.

With fewer people to cultivate the land, the Osage had difficulty producing enough food.
They also couldn't kill as many bison and deer because they were always fighting with neighbors.

Because of the illnesses and disputes, resources became more difficult to come by.

Many Osage warriors were killed in battles with invading tribes. It was a trying moment when so many people were ill as a result of the new pathogens. The Osage had to battle hard to maintain their houses and avoid starvation.

Things began to improve for the Osage by the 1720s. Despite the fact that many individuals became ill earlier, their population was expanding again. The Osage now held the majority of the land in Missour-ee.

They grew stronger by forming friendships with French colonists in America. The Osage were given firearms by French merchants.

Previously, the Osage could only hunt and battle with arrows and other implements. The Osage were considerably harder now that they had rifles from their French pals.

They could easily defeat other tribes, such as the Cherokee and Sauk, who attempted to take Osage land.

The French exchanged cannons for furs caught by the Osage. This trade was extremely beneficial to the Osage.

They could better guard their area from attackers if they had superior weaponry. Other tribes could not now take over Osage settlements.

The Osage Nation rose to prominence in Missour-ee by collaborating with French immigrants.

They controlled the majority of the area since they possessed the strongest weaponry owing to their French business partners. This restored the Osage's sense of security and safety.

More individuals began to migrate to America from England in the 1800s.

These Anglo immigrants want the land in Missour-ee where the Osage dwelt. They forced the Osage to cede large portions of their country.

The Osage felt cramped now that there were so many English settlers.

The Osage leaders decided to sell big regions to the Anglos in order to make room and receive what they needed.

This occurred in the early 1800s as an increasing number of English settlers went west.

The Osage were aware that if they did not surrender some of their holdings to the newcomers, they would lose their territories.

So, in the 1830s, the Osage moved further west. They moved to new homes in Kansas known as reserves.

This was in accordance with the formal agreements signed by Osage and Anglo officials.

The Osage were able to maintain part of their lands as a result of the relocation, but they lost a lot in Missour-ee, where their people had resided for a long time.

They had to relocate because all of the English settlers needed more space to expand their crops and communities.

By the 1850s, some Anglo settlers had discovered glittering yellow gold buried in the hills and streams of Kansas' Osage territory.

This metal's name was gold. The news of the gold discovery traveled quickly.

Thousands of newcomers flocked into Osage territory in search of gold.

They were dubbed "forty-niners" because the majority of gold hunters came in 1849.

Leavenworth and other mining towns sprung up overnight.

The Osage had never seen so many invaders on their land. The miners dug and blasted everywhere, even in Osage graveyards.

They muddied the waters and refused to leave.

Fights erupted as the miners refused to follow Osage regulations. Claim-jumpers who tried to seize their land killed some Osage men.

The Osage chiefs sought assistance from the Anglo government, but the miners persisted.

To make place for the miners, the Osage leaders agreed to sell more Kansas territory to the government.

In exchange, they were promised money and a new home in Indian Territory, which is today known as Oklahoma.

The Osage Nation relocated yet again in 1871, this time to a reserve in present-day Osage County.

The new region was far smaller than their old Missouri domain. Many Osage were dissatisfied with the relocation, but they had little option.

The Osage were given a reserve of around 1.5 million acres between the Arkansas and Verdigris rivers.

The Osage worked hard to build new dwellings and begin a new life on the prairie, hoping for peace at long last.

However, battles with European settlers and the existing Cheyenne and Arapaho tribes ensured that life was still difficult. Resources had to be shared, and occasionally disputes arose.

Over the next few decades, the Osage people gradually recovered from previous illnesses and battles.

They conformed to the reservation system while preserving their language and customs to the greatest extent possible.

While the loss of their ancestral grounds was devastating, the 1871 migration to present-day Osage County, Oklahoma gave an opportunity to rebuild their lives and country.

By this time, the Osage had incorporated elements of European-American culture and Christianity while retaining their language and customs.

As the reservation was partitioned among tribe members, they devised a system of tribal headrights for land leasing.

The Osage adapted to the reservation system and prospered via cattle ranching and farming in the late 1800s. They developed a constitution and utilized treaty revenues to finance education and economic growth.

This laid the groundwork for the discovery of oil on their grounds, which would make the Osage extremely rich in the early twentieth century. Little did they realize that the discovery of black gold beneath their new reserve would change everything - that greed and corruption would lead to the horrific killings that annihilated the tribe.

Wealth accumulation of tribal members post-oil

The Osage people were struggling to live on their Oklahoma reservation in the late 1800s. With little food or money, life was difficult. Then, in the 1900s, something incredible occurred.

Osage Nation in 1906

Underground oil was discovered on Osage grounds. The Osage were dubbed "oil Indians" by white colonists because black gold lay beneath their feet. The Osage tribe was paid by oil companies to drill for oil. Each Osage member received a part of the money, known as a "headright."

Oil in Osage

Mollie and Anna, two Osage sisters, possessed headrights. At first, the money came in little amounts.

However, gushers quickly struck, and oil revenues flowed in. Each month, the headright payments increased to be worth thousands of dollars.

Non-Indians felt envious of Osage's wealth. Whites had long accused Native Americans of being indolent, yet the Osage were suddenly the richest people in the county! Some whites were enraged to find Oil Indians living in large mansions due to greed.

Anna was the first to die, from a gunshot wound sustained in an accident in 1921. Lizzie Kyle was then poisoned.

Over the next several years, more Osage were killed in shootings, "accidents," and diseases.

Suspicions emerged that the affluent Osages were being killed for their money.

The FBI was called in to help track down the murderers who were targeting Osage "wealthy widows."

They went undercover, dug up bodies, and tracked down the money trail. It led them to William Hale and other shady whites plotting Osage's murder for their headrights.

1

Chapter

First Murder

The Murder of Anna Brown

Anna Brown, 34, was a recognized Osage tribal member and one of Lizzie Q's four daughters.

Minnie, her sister, had died three years before of what physicians described as "a peculiar wasting illness."

Minnie was just 27 years old when she died, and she had been in good health until the commencement of her perplexing sickness.

Anna was the most outgoing of the three sisters. She'd divorced Oda Brown and gone out drinking, dancing, and carousing with friends until the sun came up.

Anna's servants claimed she had "very loose morals with white men."

Anna traveled to Gray Horse on May 21, 1923, at the suggestion of her younger sister Mollie, to care for her ill mother.

However, Anna was high on bootleg whiskey, and things did not go as planned.

Bryan Burkhart, Mollie's husband Ernest's younger brother, offered to drop Anna down at her house once she sobered up and ate.

Anna kissed Mollie goodbye and followed Bryan out the door. Mollie never saw her sister after that.

Anna Kyle Brown

A week later, a child squirrel hunting at a ravine north of Fairfax discovered a rotting corpse.

The gold fillings and the blanket indicated that it had to be Anna Brown's body. An autopsy was performed by two local doctors, James and David Shoun.

Anna had been dead for almost a week, according to the autopsy, and she had been shot in the head with a .32-caliber bullet.

William Hale was a key supporter in Mollie's search for justice in the murder of her sister Anna.

Hale was Ernest Burkhart's uncle, as was his brother, Bryan Burkhart, dubbed "King of the Osage Hills."

Ernest Burkhart and his brother traveled to Oklahoma in search of work in the oil sector.

In 1912, he arrived and lived with his uncle, William Hale.

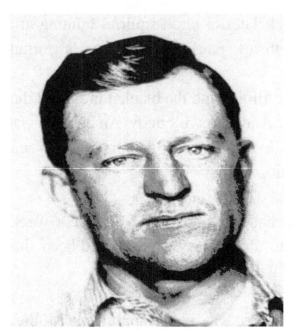

Ernest Burkhart

They lived on his ranch in Gray Horse, some 20 miles west of Pawhuska, Osage County's county seat.

Burkhart worked as a taxi driver and conducted errands for his uncle, Hale. It was in this capacity that he met his future wife, Mollie Kyle.

Mollie was Osage, but she knew English, and Ernest ultimately learned some of her language as well.

They fell in love and married in 1917, thanks to Hale's persuasion.

Hale was well-connected, affluent, and influential. He was a cattle rancher, but he also had a bank, a grocery shop, and a funeral parlor in Fairfax.

He wore his clothes neatly, had a rosy complexion, and exuded "a self-confident and military air."

In his letters, he signed himself "Rev. W. K. Hale" and described himself as a "true friend" of the Osages.

He gave money to schools and hospitals, worked as a deputy sheriff in Fairfax, owned 45,000 acres of great grazing pasture, and even recited poetry.

William K. Hale

He was the owner of a Fairfax bank and a beautiful horse stable. Hale promised Mollie that he would assist in the hunt for Anna's murderer. He called Anna a "mighty good friend."

The coroner's inquest into Anna's death yielded scanty answers.

Bryan Burkhart told inquest jurors that he dropped Anna off at her residence at "5 or 4:30" on the day of her murder and never saw her again.

Some assumed Anna's murderer came from outside the tribe, while others suspected her ex-husband, Oda Brown.

However, prosecutors lacked strong proof. Mollie's family offered a $2000 prize for information leading to Anna's killer's arrest, but no one came forward.

Hale also pledged his own incentives, both for Anna's killer and for Charles Whitehorn's killer, adding, "We've got to stop this bloody business."

Meanwhile, Lizzie, who had been awarded Anna's inheritance, became increasingly ill with what many suspected was the same mysterious wasting disease that had killed her daughter, Minnie. Lizzie died in July, two months after Anna died.

Several other Osage were slaughtered at this time, including Mollie's relatives, leaving her and her husband as the sole inheritors of their fortune.

Bill Smith, Mollie's brother-in-law, thought that Lizzie's death had nothing to do with a strange ailment.
He suspected she had been poisoned, and that Lizzie's, Minnie's, and Anna's deaths had a lot to do with the important headright in Osage oil that her family claimed.
No one was allowed to buy or sell headrights. They could, however, be inherited.

Other Osage members died under strange circumstances as detectives conducted their investigations.
William Stepson, a 21-year-old champion steer roper, collapsed and suffocated as a result of strychnine poisoning.

A month later, another Osage lady died of what was thought to be poisoning.
In August 1922, Barney McBride, a wealthy oilman trusted by the Osage, traveled to

Washington DC to request a government investigation into the Oklahoma murders.

McBride stepped outside the bar after an evening of billiards in the capital, where someone wrapped a burlap sack around his head and stabbed him nearly twenty times. McBride's murder drew widespread notice.

A headline in the Washington Post revealed what many in Oklahoma were beginning to suspect: **a conspiracy to murder wealthy Indians.**

How did Mollie Burkhart end up?

The Osage society rejected Mollie for sticking by her ex-husband until he came clean in 1926.

Mollie divorced him and wed John Cobb. In 1937, she passed away at the age of 50.

After the Great Depression, the Kyle family fortune was much diminished, and the children she had with Ernest inherited it.

The region's oil output has started to decline, and the current generation's earnings are "not enough to live on," according to Margie Burkhart, Mollie and Ernest's granddaughter.

Mollie Burkhart

2

Chapter

Second Murder

The Murder of Henry Roan

An automobile was seen descending a steep slope northwest of Fairfax, Oklahoma, in February 1923 by two hunters.

The hunters alerted the local authorities to their find, and they discovered a man's body slumped behind the wheel of the automobile.

His head had been shot in the back. Henry Roan was the 40-year-old victim. Roan had two children and was a married man.

Later, Roan was characterized by J. Edgar Hoover as "a picturesque, full-blood Osage Indian, six-foot tall and a fine looking specimen."

Naturally, Bill Hale was among the first people to learn about Roan's murder from the authorities.

Roan, according to the Fairfax mayor, "considered W. K. Hale his best friend." Hale was a pallbearer during Roan's well-attended funeral, when Osage elders sang their customary death songs.

Hale had visited Roan just a few weeks prior to Roan's death, trying to assist him in coping with the news that his wife was seeing someone called Roy Bunch.

Was it Bunch who killed the victim? Hale said he ought to be treated as a suspect at the very least.

As for Hale, he had to be considering the $25,000 he would shortly get because Roan had named him as the beneficiary of his life insurance policy.

The Osage were terrified to a whole new degree when Roan died. As they lit their dwellings in the dark, they pondered over who might come next.

Bill and Rita Smith, who made the decision to move from their remote rural house to the somewhat safer neighborhood of Fairfax, were among the concerned parties.

The Smiths, like many Osage, kept a dog for protection. However, in March 1923, pets in their area started to pass away from poisoning.

3

Chapter

Series Of Murders

Bill Smith was among the Osage who had demanded most vocally that the killings be investigated.

Some Osage said that an "evil spirit" was pursuing their community when he showed up before the Tribal Council to demand justice.

Smith exclaimed, "No!" "There is no evil spirit except one in human form."

Smith said nothing when a few people in the throng begged him to identify the murderer. Identifying the murderer or murderers would be tantamount to a death sentence.

On March 9, Bill Smith drove his Studebaker back to his Fairfax home with a buddy after looking into an investigation lead about Roan's death.

Rita, his wife, was there to greet him. Nettie Brookshire, their seventeen-year-old white servant, was also staying the night at the Smith residence.

A thunderous explosion completely destroyed the Smith home at 2:50 in the morning. Rita and Nettie passed away very immediately, but Bill Smith, surprisingly, lived for a few days despite being nearly completely burnt.

Smith would scream out, "They got Rita and now it looks like they got me," as he was on the verge of death.

The Tribal Chieftain declared, "We must appeal to the white father in Washington," following the Smith killings.

Once content and quiet, our people now fear for their lives.When he will be summoned to the Happy Hunting Grounds is unknown."

In a resolution approved by the Tribal Council, it was requested that *"the Honorable Secretary of the Interior be requested to obtain the services of the Department of Justice in capturing and prosecuting the murderers of the members of the Osage tribe."*

4

Chapter

The Investigation

The explosion made the hunt for the murderers even more urgent, but many Osage saw corruption everywhere and were unsure of whom to believe.

W. V. Vaughan, a local lawyer and former prosecutor, made every effort to solve the crimes.

Vaughan was informed in June 1923 that George Bigheart, an Osage member, was suspected of poisoning and was dying in an Oklahoma City hospital.

Bigheart possessed knowledge on the killings. (It's quite likely that Bigheart and Hale had seen each other just before Bigheart started to deteriorate and needed to be brought to the hospital.)

Bigheart trusted no one else and would only divulge his insights to Vaughan.

To see Bigheart, Vaughan hurried to Oklahoma City.

Following Bigheart's death in his care, Vaughan called the Osage County sheriff to notify him that he was taking the first train out of the county and that he had fresh, crucial information on the Osage homicides.

Vaughan's corpse was found north of Oklahoma City, close to train tracks, thirty-six hours later.

He had been hurled from the train, naked, and had a fractured neck.

Tom White, the director of the Bureau's Houston office, was called to Washington in the summer of 1925 by J. Edgar Hoover, the thirty-year-old new leader of the Bureau of

Investigation (later to be better known as the FBI).

White was known for his skill and honesty, and Hoover had given him a significant assignment.

He requested that he oversee the Bureau's investigation into the Osage killings, which had started in 1923.

Situation described by Hoover as *"acute and delicate."*

Due to his previous background, the position put him at a substantial personal danger of death or serious injury and required him to relocate his family to Oklahoma City in order to oversee the field office.

"I am human enough and ambitious enough to want" the position, White said to Hoover.

After taking over the investigation, White went through a ton of case files.

Agents had focused on the cases they thought had the most chance of being resolved and prosecuted—namely, the killings of Henry Roan, Anna Brown, and Charles Whitehorn, as well as the bombing murders of Bill and Rita Smith and their servant.

It has been a challenging study. As might be expected, practically everyone with knowledge was unwilling to divulge for fear of being the next casualty of the murders.

Almost all of the agents, with the exception of White, worked covertly as prospectors, cattlemen, "medicine men," and insurance salespeople.

The Bureau characterizes "the general class of the citizenry in the territory" as "very low" in a 1953 history of the Osage murder trials.

In addition to an abundance of oil, the wealthy oil fields gave rise to prostitution, gambling, corruption, easy money, prostitutes, whiskey, and parasites who were out to fleece the Indian of everything he possessed.

Osage mistrust of white people was "virtually universal," according to the FBI investigation, and "agents had to rebuild their confidence in law enforcement."

Before it yielded results, the Anna Brown murder inquiry created further questions.

Why was there no bullet discovered during the autopsy if there was no exit wound in the front of Anna's skull?

Could David and James Shoun, the examining physicians, have taken it?

What about the claim made by an Indian lady from Kaw that Rose Osage murdered Anna because she made an attempt to woo his boyfriend?

However, Rose Osage's alibi held up, and the Kaw Indian's account fell flat.

Why would she mislead detectives?

Is she being paid to keep the real murderer safe?

When an old farmer informed investigators he had seen Anna the night before she was killed, it was the first big development in the Anna Brown case.

She was seated in a vehicle that had pulled up to a Ralston hotel. She greeted a member of his group.

Crucial details were also provided by the farmer's wife. Bryan Burkhart was the guy behind the wheel.

She claimed that as they backed away from the curb, Burkhart went "straight west from there."

Agents were aware that Burkhart said he had left Anna at her house at "5 or 4:30" and had not seen her alive again.

Burkhart was lying if the farm couple was correct.

After compiling data from various sources, the agents started to construct a chronology that showed Burkhart, Anna, and an unnamed "third man" attending a speakeasy until about one in the morning.

Around three in the morning, according to another witness, Bryan was yelling at Anna, telling her to "get in this car" and stop her folly.

When Bryan Burkhart did eventually make it back home, it was just before dawn.

A further hiccup in the inquiry occurred when a private investigator, purportedly employed by W. K. Hale was taken into custody for robbery in Tulsa.

Agents were informed by the "private eye" that Hale had really employed him to "shape an alibi" by locating witnesses who would tell lies.

He provided yet another insightful tip.

He added that Ernest Burkhart was frequently present when he met with Hale and Bryan

Burkhart to talk about his muddying-the-waters strategy.

Tom White conducted interviews with those who had visited Bill Smith in the hospital room in the final four days before he passed away from explosion-related injuries.

Although Smith's lawyer said that Smith had informed him as Smith lay in his hospital bed, *"You know, I only had two enemies in the world,"* Hale and Ernest Burkhart, no one he spoke to indicated Smith had really named his killers.

Furthermore, Smith's nurse disclosed that Hale had paid her a visit and asked if Smith had identified his probable murderers.

White saw a potential crucial clue to that murder in the $25,000 insurance policy that Hale possessed for Henry Roan's life.

The policy gave a clear reason. Agents were informed by an insurance salesman that Hale's claim was untrue, since Roan had insisted on designating Hale, a close friend, as his beneficiary.

The salesperson said that Hale had really requested the policy.

"Hells bells, that's just like spearing fish in a keg," Hale had said to him.

Subsequent research indicated that Hale needed to find a physician who would authorize Roan for the coverage.

Many medical professionals would be reluctant to approve a man who has a history of binge drinking and a drunk driving accident.

However, Dr. James Shoun agreed to grant the medical clearance.

White discovered one other intriguing link between Hale and Roan.

A planned reform in the legislation permitting such purchases had failed, thus Hale's prior effort to buy Roan's headright was never completed.

Additionally, White started to connect the dots between the deaths of Smith and Brown.

Since Anna was the first victim—an unmarried woman without children—her headright was transferred to her mother Lizzie, who is still alive.

Following Lizzie's death, which was most likely caused by poisoning, her two surviving children, Rita and Mollie, inherited her headright.

The final surviving sister, Mollie, would become the only heir to Rita and Bill's headrights if they were to die at the same time, as they almost did in the explosion.

Of course, Mollie was also married to Hale's nephew, Ernest Burkhart.

White pondered whether Ernest and Mollie's 1919 marriage may have been the catalyst for a protracted and deadly scheme.

The explosives expert who created the bomb that detonated the Smith residence, sometimes known as the "soup man," was identified to White by an informant.

The individual went by Asa Kirby.

But Kirby was dead, and it appeared that Hale was also responsible for Kirby's passing—another possible witness eliminated.

When Kirby tried to steal jewels from a jewelry store, he was slain.

William Hale had told the store about the intended heist, so when Kirby arrived, the shopkeeper was prepared with a shotgun.

As it turned out, Hale had even planned the heist, informing Kirby about the diamond stockpile and advising when it would be most advantageous to rob them.

Not exactly ideal for Kirby.

Mollie told a priest in the fall of 1925 that she thought someone was attempting to poison her.

Mollie had been receiving shots from the Shoun brothers that she thought were insulin, but instead of getting better, her condition was becoming worse.

Her sickness was deemed "very suspicious" by White and other agents, who made arrangements for her to be treated in a hospital.

Her health significantly improved once she stopped receiving "insulin injections" from the Shoun brothers.

The report of an agent said, "*It is an established fact that when she was removed from the control of Hale and Burkhart, she immediately regained her health.*"

When questioned thereafter on the injections he gave Mollie, James Shoun remained evasive.

Prosecutor: "*Weren't you giving her insulin?*"

"*Perhaps I was,*" Shoun said.

The Department of Justice was persuaded to take action due to a number of issues, including

Mollie's sickness and the Osage community's dread and impatience.

On January 4, 1926, warrants were issued for the arrest of Hale and Ernest Burkhart for the murders of Bill and Rita Smith and Nettie Brookshire.

Hale declined to speak with the media about his case while en route to Guthrie, Oklahoma, jail, instead choosing to remark, *"I'll not try my case in the newspapers, but in the courts of this country."*

White and Agent Frank Smith interrogated Burkhart in Guthrie in an attempt to get a confession.

They brought Blackie Thompson, an outlaw in jail, to Guthrie.

Thompson informed Burkhart that he had informed the agents that Burkhart had demanded a new car from him, along with Bill Smith's murder.

Afterwards, Burkhart made the decision to speak.

Burkhart claimed that at first, he was against the idea of blowing up the Smith residence.

However, he remarked, *"Hale brought up the fact that his wife would receive the additional funds from the inherited headrights, and I relied on Uncle Bill's judgment."*

Burkhart claimed that after attempting to persuade Blackie Thompson to perform the task, Hale turned to Asa Kirby.

"Acie would do it, that's what Hale told me." Burkhart said that Hale instructed him to convey a message to John Ramsey, a robber and bootlegger, just before Hale left for Texas.

It was a notice that it was time to end the Smith job.

When the explosion occurred, Burkhart declared, *"I knew what it was."*

Burkhart also named Ramsey as the murderous triggerman of Henry Roan.

Following Burkhart's admission, White sent agents to pick up Ramsey and place him under arrest.

Ramsey replied, *"I guess it's my neck now,"* after seeing Burkhart's signed declaration.

Ramsey acknowledged killing Roan in his confession, calling it *"a little job Hale wanted done."*

He claimed to have told Roan about sipping whiskey while perched on his car's running board.

When *"the Indian got in his car to leave, I shot him in the back of the head."* Ramsey gave the impression that Indians were not really human.

He informed the police that *"white people in Oklahoma thought no more of killing an Indian than they did in 1724."*

While Burkhart did not name his brother Bryan as a suspect in Anna Brown's murder, he did name the "third man" who was observed with Anna just before she was killed.

The man turned out to be Kelsie Morrison, a person the agents had recruited to assist them in uncovering the truth about the very crime he had taken part in.

Burkhart said that Morrison was the person who killed Anna. There was still one more individual whom the authorities needed to interrogate.

At last, White felt it was time to speak with Hale. *"We have unquestionably signed statements that implicate you as the principal in the Henry Roan and Smith family murders,"*

White informed Hale. *"We have proof to hold you guilty."*

In response, Hale said, *"I'll fight it."*

And he probably believed he would prevail in that battle. He was powerful and wealthy.

5

Chapter

FBI Report

One of the most intricate and challenging investigations the FBI has ever undertaken was the one into the Osage Indian killings that took place in the early 1920s.

The whole Osage Indian tribe and the white residents of Osage County, Oklahoma, were terrified and afraid for their lives just before the FBI's inquiry got underway after two dozen Osage Indians died inexplicably.

As a result, the tribal council adopted a resolution asking the federal government for assistance in investigating these killings.

Many people believe that the Osage Indian nation, which is located in the northeastern region of Oklahoma in the Osage hills, is the best cattle-grazing region in the world.

It is a gorgeous, rolling region with tall, green limestone grass.

That wasn't always the case. Considered to have spent $1,200,000 to purchase a poor burial for the tribe, the Osage tribe was compelled to relocate from Kansas to what became Osage County.

On July 8, 1866, the Cherokee Treaty took possession of the territory from the Cherokee Indians.

Osage County, Oklahoma, and the Osage Indian Reservation share a million and a half acres of Indian-allotted territory.

Greater than the State of Delaware, Osage County is the biggest county in the state.

It stretches from Tulsa, Oklahoma, on the south to Ponca City, Oklahoma, on the north, a distance of around sixty miles, and is bordered on the southwest by the Arkansas River.

At its broadest point, it spans sixty miles as well.

At the time of the killings, Osage County and the surrounding area had extremely untamed areas of land that were heavily forested with lumber that wasn't fit for commercial use.

Due to its nearly impassable gorges, this location provided great concealment for the several infamous crooks that set up shop there.

The Osage Indians' immense wealth served as a major draw for a variety of desperate criminals who flocked to the region from all over the nation during the killings that took place between 1921 and 1923.

An interview conducted by a Special Agent with a criminal a few years after the killings serves as a good example of the criminal milieu prevalent in the region at this time.

While incarcerated at the Oklahoma State Penitentiary, the bandit remembered that around the time of the killings, he had gone to a meeting in the Osage Country woods with thirty-two well-known bank bandits and train thieves who were running from the law.

The prisoner said that because proficiency with a handgun was a requirement for their line of work, they frequently practiced their firearm handling during their stay.

The Federal Government passed a statute on June 28, 1906, stipulating that each of the 2,229 tribe members would get an equal number of shares, or head rights.

Regardless of the tribe's population growth or decline, the number of head rights was constant. In other words, an Osage Indian born after June 28, 1906, would only be entitled to the head rights equal to his ancestors.

Numerous Osage Indians received income from or were granted large areas of land according to their head rights.

Each Osage Indian was originally given a property consisting of 160 acres.

Later, more land grants were added to this, bringing the total amount of head right allotments to around 657 acres per head.

The Osage Indian Agency oversaw the Osage Indians' affairs and handled the payment of payments owed to them.

Its headquarters were located at Pawhuska, Oklahoma.

The Osage tribe became the richest people in the world per capita when oil was found on their reserve later on.

As of June 30, 1920, there were 5,859 active producing oil wells on the reserve.

By June 30, 1922, there were 8,579 people on the rolls.

Almost every piece of land inside the reservation was leased for the extraction of natural gas or oil.

The Osage Indians received funding in a different way than other tribes since all proceeds from the land were placed in a common pool and distributed among all Indians in the tribe who qualified for allocation rights.

Indians who were deemed competent in managing their own financial affairs were granted certificates of competency, which allowed them to dispose of their assigned land holdings and head rights as they saw appropriate.

Indians who were deemed incapable of managing their finances were assigned a guardian to assist them.

Each Osage Indian eligible to receive income from the common fund received a net per capita yearly payment of $10.50 in 1880; by 1933, that amount had increased to $12,400.

However, neither the tribes nor any individual member can be claimed to have benefited from the accumulation of this wealth.

It was consoling, but it also brought sickness, immorality, human parasites, and a horrifying luxury.

It was not unusual for many Osages to have monthly grocery bills of $500 to $1,000.

Members of the tribe were given contemporary homes with all the amenities, *"only to have them roll into their blankets and sleep in the yard."*

When the Indians weren't traveling the countryside in their cars, they would often spend a lot of time in the wigwams or canopies that were located outside of many of the dwellings.

The tribe had stomp dances many times a year, and other Indian tribe members were invited to participate as guests.

Individuals and the various tribes traded gifts with one another.

The Indians would dress in colorful clothes and dance in a circle to the tom-tom's rhythmic beat during these stomp dances, which served as the reason for all-night and all-day feasts.

Following the dance, they would retire to continue dining while the audience was entertained by professional Indian dancers.

The elder men and women of the tribes joined in on this dance in addition to the youthful and energetic members.

Fullblood Osage Indian marriages were formally consummated in accordance with tribe traditions.

Every two years, the Osage Indians chose the Chief, Assistant Chief, and eight Tribal Councilmen as their tribal authorities.

In 1901, the craze for oil had already drawn dishonest prospectors to the county.

Soon after, about 2,000 Osages encountered the same issue that had driven the Indians out of other regions of the nation: the white man's attempt to take everything the Indians owned.

A man whose thirst for wealth and power was unrestrained was William K. Hale, later dubbed the *"King of the Osage,"* an uneducated and somewhat uncivilized Texas cowpuncher with a dominant demeanor, among the many daring prospectors and other white men who drifted into the Osage territory.

Hale had a captivating appearance despite his average size. He had a reddish complexion and was well-groomed.

With his shoulders back and chest out, he had a military aura of confidence and self-assurance.

Hale was able to get ownership of 5,000 acres outright and manage 45,000 acres of prime Osage grazing property through leases.

Through his interactions with the Osage Indians, he amassed enormous money.

He finally became a billionaire and possessed a stable full of exquisite horses.

In Fairfax, Oklahoma, he was the owner of a bank and had a stake in a business.

In the middle of his vast properties was a ranch house close to Grayhorse, Oklahoma, and a residence in Fairfax, Oklahoma.

He was a powerful figure in local politics and didn't appear to be able to face consequences for the numerous crimes committed against him.

His way of consolidating his position of authority and status was to obligate others through gifts or favors.

As a result, he had a large following in the area that included many well-meaning and decent residents in addition to the drifter element that had strayed in.

Hale once supposedly insured 30,000 acres of his land for $1 per acre, after which his cowboys put the grass on the property on fire one night.

Hale thus received $30,000 from the insurance coverage.Ernest Burkhart, Hale's nephew, and Bryan Burkhart, who either accompanied Hale to Osage or joined him thereafter, worked for Hale and were totally under his control.

Hale occasionally employed a lot of risky individuals, many of whom were notorious assassins for a fee and were either ex-convicts or fugitives from the law.

Lizzie Q (real name: Lizzie Kile) was an Osage squaw who was already elderly and not in good health in 1920.

The estimated estate of Lizze Q was $200,000.

Her three daughters were named Rita, Ann, and Mollie.

In the Osage, Anna was a notoriously dissolute person. She preferred white guys, and she occasionally had relationships with several of them.

She had previously been wed to a white guy named Odie Brown. Ann's estate was estimated at $100,000 in 1920.Rita stayed with her husband, a white man named William E. Smith, until her death.

The nephew of Hale, Ernest Burkhart, married Mollie.

Mollie seems to have been Hale's chosen conduit for obtaining the family's possessions through the Burkharts.

Although Anna had some personal relationship with one of the Burkhart sons, it seems that her notoriety prevented even the Burkharts from getting married.

However, Anna Brown was wealthy, and the stakes were high.

The elderly mother Lizzie Q was transferred to Ernest Burkhart's Grayhorse residence in 1920, where she resided with her daughter Mollie.

In the grand scheme of things, she was the second member of the family to be put under Hale's direct control.

Lizzie Q was diagnosed with a disease early in 1921 that was clearly going to cause her death.

She had been coerced into signing a will, which mostly bequeathed her possessions to Ernest Burkhart's spouse and kids.

However, the stakes were much larger to win.

Lizzie Q's wealth would grow by half of Anna Brown's legacy if the elderly woman were to survive, according to state law.

However, the majority of Anna's inheritance would be directed into collateral if she were to outlive her mother.

The severely decomposed and bloated body of Anna Brown was discovered on May 27, 1921, by a hunting party in a gully near the Pawhuska–Fairfax Road, three miles from Fairfax, Oklahoma.

It seemed like she had been dead for a week or two.

The deceased woman was barefoot, with a white undershirt and a blue broadcloth shirt on.

A few feet from the bank was a shawl that looked to be hers.An undertaker arrived and took control of the body after the hunters alerted him right away.

The body was nearly bursting with decay and swelling.

A bullet hole was found in the back of the head, slightly to the left of the middle and entering the skull bone, and the scalp slid off the skull as the body was being prepared for burial.

No escape hole was discovered.

Only a rudimentary and hurried autopsy was conducted because of the body's awful stench and state, which involved splitting the skull in half from front to back and looking for the bullet inside the decomposing brain matter.

It seems that none was discovered.

The inquiry into Anna Brown's death was launched very once, and W. E. Smith, her brother-in-law, was the family member that pursued it the most.

He and his spouse were adamant in their conviction that Bill Hale and his nephews were accountable for the killing.

After being detained and accused of killing Anna Brown in state courts, Bryan Burkhart was freed thanks to Hale's provision of a bail.

Half of Ann's fortune was added to Lizzie Q's estate upon Anna's passing.

Two months after Anna Brown's death, Lizzie Q died away at the residence of her daughter, Mollie Burkhart, who was Ernest Burkhart's wife.

This was the next anticipated event. So the Burkharts received the majority of Lizzie Q's fortune as well as half of Anna Brown's wealth.

Henry Roan is a charming full-blooded Osage Indian relative of Anna Brown.
Standing six feet tall, with his hair styled down his back in plaits, he was a handsome example of an Osage masculinity.

Roan was residing in Fairfax, Oklahoma, in January 1923 with his full-blooded Osage wife Mary and their kids.
An ardent drinker, Roan would often go on drinking binges that may last up to four weeks at a time.

Thus, there was no commotion when he vanished from view for a few days.

A few miles northwest of Fairfax, on February 6, 1923, an Indian child discovered a vehicle in a rocky swale, approximately 200 yards off the back road between Fairfax and Burbank.

After the child raced to Fairfax, he came back with two police officers and they discovered Roan's body on the front seat of his car.

The bullet wound in his head suggested that it had entered just behind his left ear and broken the windshield glass, which had been scattered across the right eye and for approximately twenty feet back along the automobile tracks.

There were still glass fragments on the car's hood.

With his feet barely off the pedals and his head resting on the right side of the seat with his cap tucked beneath it, Roan was laying on the front seat.

The way the corpse was positioned made it obvious that Roan was operating a vehicle when he was shot.

It appeared that the person had been deceased for ten days or so. When it was discovered, it had been frozen solid at first, but it had started to melt and decay.

It was noted that the weather was quite chilly from January 26 to February 3 or 4, which is why it is thought that the roan was killed on January 26.

Bill Hale offered to pay for a $25,000 insurance policy on Henry Roan's life not long after Roan passed away.

Hale filed a lawsuit in federal court when the insurance company refused to pay the indemnity on the basis of fraud and deception.

Regarding this, a review of the different court documents revealed that Roan had applied for the appointment of a guardian in the District Court of Osage County and that, at the time, he owed Hale $6,000, which was the remaining amount on a Fairfax home.

There was no indication of more debt.

The only person who opposed Roan was Dave Belnap, a worthless white man who had been seeing Roan's wife for a while before getting married a few months after Roan passed away.

Hale tried to take advantage of this animosity by spreading a tale that Belnap was the cause of the demise.

Agents subsequently had to carry out a thorough investigation in order to establish Belnap's innocence.

Agents were forced to undertake unnecessary travels to California, New Mexico, Old Mexico, Kansas, Colorado, Texas, and Arizona as a result of other untrue rumors and comments made by Hale and his numerous pals and goons.

E. Smith, Rita's husband and Anna Brown's brother-in-law, shared a cozy house with his spouse and Nettie Brookshire, a white domestic worker.

In addition to letting Hale know that he had evidence linking him to Anna Brown's death, Smith had maintained his active investigation into the case and had become quite hostile with Hale after demanding that Hale give him $5,000 that he claimed he was owed.

Hale declined to make the payment.

An explosion destroyed Smith's Fairfax house at around 2:50 A.M. on March 10, 1923, less than two months after Henry Roan's body was discovered.

The bodies of his wife Rita and their 17-year-old white servant Nettie Brookshire were blown apart in an instant.

Later, 300 feet away, pieces of their flesh were discovered plastered on a home.

After being pulled from the wreckage, Smith lived there for around four days before passing away.

In his final statement, he declared that Hale and the Burkhart family were the only adversaries he had who he might accuse of blowing up his house.

Witnesses saw the home flare up once or twice a second or two before the explosion, suggesting that it had been saturated on one or more sides with kerosene or something similar.

On the north side, it quickly caught fire and burned almost completely.

The home included a 5-inch-thick concrete floor in the basement garage.

The explosion shattered the concrete floor in the center, creating a hole that was about five feet in diameter and three feet deep.

For a while, the ruin of what had once been a house stood as a terrifying monument to Hale and his friends.

Mollie Burkhart, Ernest's wife, was the sole surviving member of Lizzie's family following the death of Rita Smith.

Since Mollie Burkhart was Rita Smith's only surviving sister, this triple murder was calculated to further enrich the Ernest Burkhart family by approximately $150,000 from Rita Smith's estate.

This was in addition to wiping out Smith's $6,000 claim against Hale and eliminating a man eager to see the Hale-Burkhart conspiracy brought to justice.

However, Rita and her husband had created a joint will that avoided this, stating that the survivor would inherit the estate of the first to pass away.

All of the property passed to Smith, who outlived Rita by around four days, then, upon his death, to a girl who was Smith's daughter from a previous marriage who lived in Arkansas without knowing Hale or the Burkharts.

The FBI began looking into these horrific killings in 1923, and over the next several years, they painstakingly pieced together the puzzle and gathered evidence from around the nation that would allow the guilty persons to be found guilty.

Special Agents showed unwavering bravery and tenacity in the face of seemingly insurmountable hurdles.

They were carefully chosen because of their familiarity with Indian and frontier life.

Numerous leads, many intended to mislead them and divert them from the genuine culprits' trail, led them to drive hundreds of miles across the oil fields day and night in the heat, cold, rain, snow, and muck.

The fact that many of the key witnesses had fled the nation, leaving no address and, in many cases, were wanted for crimes, posed another significant challenge.

Private investigators had been working on the cases for months, interviewing a great number of people—many of whom had been paid by the murders themselves to thwart the inquiry.

Many of these investigators were too forthcoming in discussing the information they had obtained, which made many of the people they interrogated reticent and unpleasant.

Furthermore, the fact that the people had promised incentives for the killings' solution drew a lot of amateur investigators, which made the FBI's job much more difficult.

In fact, the law-abiding residents were afraid to talk to the agents about the killings for fear that the killers would find out they had said something and then kill them.

They were no longer hopeful that the killings would ever result in any action. FBI agents needed to regain faith in the legal system.

The territory's overall populace belonged to a very low social level.

In addition to an abundance of oil, the lucrative oil fields gave rise to prostitutes, gambling, corruption, easy money, whiskey, and parasites who were out to deprive the Indian of everything he possessed.

Consequently, dread and mistrust of the white man were nearly prevalent among the Indians themselves.

As a result, the majority of them were reluctant to discuss the killings with FBI agents.

In order to get out of this predicament, a few of the agents went undercover as prospectors, cattlemen, insurance salespeople, and Indian *"medicine men."*

Under the guise of a *"medicine man,"* the agent stated he was looking for relatives who had relocated to Oklahoma a few years prior.

The Indians welcomed him with open arms when he produced medicine, which was primarily made of sweetened water.

He was able to win their cooperation and confidence by using this channel.

He attended their rituals and paid them visits, learning a great deal of important information regarding the killings.

In the inner circle and tribal councils, he also performed the role of *"medicine man,"* assisting the Osages in problem-solving and formulating plans for running their tribal government.

By posing as an insurance salesperson, the agent was able to enter people's houses and get information that they were afraid to discuss with government agents because they were afraid of Bill Hale.

In the process, the agent sold valid insurance policies.

The many facets of the murder cases were frequently directly impacted by the facts discovered in relation to the insurance plans themselves.

William Hale was even approached by this agent, who nearly convinced him to buy an insurance policy.

After meeting Hale for the first time at a motel in Fairfax, Oklahoma, this agent saw him many times.

The agent discovered that Hale was rather open about his childhood and his cattle trades, including how he fled his family and became a cowboy.

Hale was known for having an extremely high opinion of himself and for being both *"woman crazy"* and *"money mad."*

Fearful, Hale told the agent he had been experiencing stomach problems and was having problems falling asleep.

He stated that he had sold all of his cattle interests, leaving him with only 250 head of cattle and around 75 tons of cottonseed cakes.

He added that he was unsure of his specific plans but that he thought he needed a protracted vacation.

It was discovered by the Agent that Hale had already made $75,000 from his cattle transactions and other interests that year (1925).

Hale showed the undercover agent around to a number of notable Fairfax residents and was quite cordial with him.

The Agent discovered that Hale was running a disinformation operation to gain as many allies as possible.

He bought them suits, co-signed messages for others, gave them several gifts to different people, gave little boys horses, and was incredibly kind to the elderly and ill.

The Agent discovered that Hale had informed a tailor he was planning a vacation to Florida when he placed an order for a new suit and an overcoat.

He also found out that Hale's eighteen-year-old daughter had mentioned that the family was ready to go at any time, with everything packed.

In front of the undercover agent, Hale declared to the others that he was sick of two-bit criminals taking advantage of his notoriety and that he was too cunning and eager to go cold.

A second undercover agent, posing as a typical Texas cowboy, cultivated strong relationships with several of Hale's associates and staff members, many of whom unwittingly provided important intelligence.

Because there were so many thieves and murders in the neighborhood, the agents' lives while they were looking into these killings were in constant risk.

Undercover agents frequently got together late at night in isolated and hazardous locations around Osage County, like the woods that Al Spencer used as a meeting spot and as a hideout for his infamous gang of bank robbers, and Dead Man's Hill, where numerous murders and robberies had been planned.

W. K. Hale sought to recruit Spencer to kill Indians, as the agents discovered.

At Hale's trial, additional Spencer ring members testified that Hale had also made an unsuccessful attempt to recruit them to kill certain Indians.

At one point, at William Hale's encouragement, a nephew of Hale approached "Curley" Johnson, another bank robber operating in this region, with the intention of employing Johnson to kill several Indians.

Johnson was subsequently slain inexplicably, and it was widely believed that Hale had ordered his death out of concern that Johnson may *talk.*

Hale and Henry Grammer, two more infamous criminals who controlled the Osage liquor trade, were the leaders of Osage County's criminal element.

A privately owned power plant, where a group of criminal fugitives from all over the United States labored day and night to make illicit booze, is said to have been the means by which he kept some of the forests around his farm lighted.

Prior to the FBI's probe, Grammer passed away in a car accident, and he had $15,000 in cash on him when he passed away.

There was a large wound beneath his left armpit, and there were rumors that the person who murdered him was a criminal who was with him when the accident happened.

According to information gleaned by an FBI agent, the criminals would get an Indian drunk, have a doctor check him out, declare him inebriated, and then give him a hypodermic injection of morphine in connection with the unexplained deaths of a significant number of Indians.

Following the doctor's departure, the gang members would fatally inject the inebriated Indian beneath his armpit with a massive quantity of morphine.

The following would appear on the doctor's certificate: *"Death from alcoholic poisoning."*

Burt Lawson, a prisoner housed in the Oklahoma State Penitentiary in McAlester, Oklahoma, made many admissions to the killings, alleging that Hale had hired him to kill W. E. Smith and his family, which further complicated the FBI's investigation into these killings.

Upon meticulous inquiry by Special Agents, it was discovered that Hale had fabricate this tale on his own, well aware that he could provide Lawson with an ideal alibi while also clearing his own name.

Agents had to spend many exhausting hours reviewing Lawson's confessions in order to determine the actual facts of the case, all because of his admissions.

Coincidentally, Lawson revealed himself to be a glutton who consumed T-bone steak and French-fried potatoes three times a day while under the protection of FBI agents.

When Lawson first went to a cafeteria with Agents, he protested to the cashier that he didn't have enough place for a meat dish despite having four pieces of pie and three pieces of cake on his tray.

Agents discovered that in 1920, Ernest Burkhart gave a criminal an explanation of why he wanted Bill Smith and his wife killed: both Mrs. Smith and his wife were sisters; their mother was elderly, very ill, and likely to pass away at any time; if the elderly woman passed away first, Smith's wife would inherit a portion of her estate; if Mrs. Smith died first, Ernest's wife would inherit the majority of her wealth upon her death.

Burkhart promised the culprits that in exchange for their crimes, they could steal the Smiths of their diamonds and receive a Buick car worth $1,000.

Agents received word on March 4, 1024, that the Indian women of Ernest and Bryan Burkhart were very afraid for their life and were considering leaving their husbands behind with their children.

They planned to employ a personal guard once they moved out to avoid getting murdered over their belongings.

Agents were informed that Joe Bigheart, an Osage Indian, and his spouse Bertha had adopted the youngest of Ernest Burkhart's children, a newborn girl called Anna, in honor of Anna Brown.

Joe Bigheart passed away after this adoption, leaving the Burkhart kid with half of his wealth, which was estimated to be worth $75,000 or more.

Since Bertha and Joe Bigheart were childless, the kid would also be entitled to half of Bertha Bigheart's wealth, which was estimated to be worth $150,000.

There was talk at the time that Bertha Bigheart and her parents were going to be eliminated by the Hale-Burkhart group in order to give the adopted kid the entire estate.

One of the women who had worked for Anna Brown told the agents that on May 21, 1921, while she was at home, Anna Brown received a call asking her to come to Grayhorse to see her extremely sick mother.

She packed her handbag with personal belongings and departed her house at eight in the morning in a taxi.

When Ann's slain corpse was discovered on May 27, 1921, this woman went to her home.

She discovered that it was unlocked and in the same state as when Anna had left early that morning.

There was no indication of any disruption or usage of the beds.

But Ann's purse, which she had brought with her, was still there.

This suggested that the bag had been returned by Anna or another person.

According to a domestic worker in Ernest Burkhart's house, on May 21, Anna Brown was picked up by a taxicab so she could see her mother.

During the day, Anna drank and argued with Bryan Burkhart, her mother, and her sister Mollie.

Anna drank in the summer house for the most of the day.

This lady said that Anna had threatened to murder any woman she caught flirting with Bryan because she was envious of him.

The same lady had been told by Bryan that Anna had threatened to murder him if he didn't marry her, but that he would kill her first.

This domestic said that at around 2:00 PM, the Burkhart men took the kids to a horse race at Grayhorse, and they didn't come back until 5:30 or 5:00 PM.

That day, Anna stayed at the residence of Ernest Burkhart.

Around 5:30 p.m., supper was served, and every Burkhart man was there.

But Anna stayed in the summer home and pouted, refusing to eat.

Anna was taken by the Burkhart guys as they departed at around 7:00 P.M.

It was possible to track down another witness, who testified that on May 21, 1921, he had met Bryan Burkhart and Anna Brown in a whiskey establishment west of Rolston.

They agreed to meet again at another roadhouse three miles northeast of Burbank.

They stayed at this business until 10:00 P.M. and then left.

This second roadhouse, three miles northeast of Burbank, was where the party stayed.

The group remained at this second roadhouse until perhaps 12:30 in the morning.

He said that additional partygoers were in the second automobile, while Bryan Burkhart, Anna Brown, and another person were in Ernest Burkhart's vehicle.

They continued to another roadhouse two miles east of Burbank, where they stayed in their car after purchasing some whisky in pop bottles.

The two cars continued toward Fairfax, he claimed, but at a split in the road approximately one mile northeast of Fairfax, one drove east and the other, carrying Bryan Burkhart, Anna, and a third person, headed west.

It was thought to be Sunday, May 22, around 2:00 A.M.

This witness stated that he had heard Hale, Bryan, and the third person discussing the murder of Anna Brown that May 21st, and that he was aware that Bill Hale had given Bryan Burkhart the .32 caliber revolver he needed to shoot her that evening.

Subsequent inquiry showed that Bryan Burkhart and neat-appearing white guy Kelsey Morrison, who was joined by Morrison's fullblood Osage wife, had loaded Anna with alcohol the night before she was murdered.

They passed William K. Hale's ranch house, where Hale had given Morrison an automatic weapon with a.32 caliber so he could shoot Anna.

The group left Hale's house and drove to a location just a few hundred feet from the body's eventual discovery.

As Bryan Burkhart restrained an inebriated Anna, Morrison shot her in the back of the head.

Morrison admitted that he had killed Anna at Hale's request.

At Hale's trial, Morrison attested to these facts, which were supported by his wife and a bootlegger who claimed on the witness stand to have witnessed Anna Brown's murder while transporting liquor that Burkhart and Morrison had ordered.

Hale had hired John Ramsey, a 50-year-old bootlegger and typical rough-and-tumble western criminal who had served a prison sentence for cattle rustling, to kill Henry Roan, William E. Smith, Rita Smith, and Nettie Brookshire, according to an FBI inquiry.

It came to light that Hale had been given John Ramsey by Henry Grammer as the murderer.

Prior to the Roan murder, Hale gave Ramsey $500 toward a Ford automobile as part of the deal, and after the murder, he gave Ramsey $1,000 in cash.

When John Ramsey killed Roan, he had just been shown who the Indian Hale wanted slain on the streets of Fairfax, Oklahoma; he did not even know Roan's name.

Because of Roan's love of whisky, Ramsey became friends with him and brought him out on multiple occasions, pretending to give him alcohol but really killing him.

Each time, Ramsey lost courage, but on January 26, 1923, he convinced Roan to take a car all the way to the bottom of a canyon.

Here, out of sight of the surrounding road, he used a .45 caliber revolver that he had taken from Henry Grammer's arsenal to shoot Roan in the back of the head.

Later, Hale vented his fury, claiming that Ramsey had intended to shoot Roan in the back of the head in order to give the impression that he had committed suicide.

At Roan's burial, Hale volunteered to be a pallbearer, and Ramsey feigned to be very moved when he saw the body.

The admissions of Ernest Burkhart, who attended all of the murder-related talks, and Ramsey supported the details surrounding Roan's murder.

Investigations revealed that Hale paid John Ramsey $1,600 after hiring Asa "Ace" Kirby and Ramsey to kill William E. Smith and his wife. Acting on orders from his uncle, Ernest Burkhart showed Kirby and Ramsey the location of the Smiths' home.

The day of the murder, he went looking for Ramsey and informed him that, in an effort to dispel suspicion, Hale and Henry Grammer were heading to a cattlemen's convention in Fort Worth, Texas, and that the Smiths were to be killed that evening.

Agents discovered that a five-gallon nitroglycerin keg had been lit on fire and hidden beneath the Smith home.

Agents also discovered that Hale had tried to hire infamous outlaw Al Spencer to kill the Smiths, but Spencer had turned him down. Spencer claimed he had no qualms about blowing up a safe or robbing a train, killing people while doing so, but he had not gone so far as to kill defenseless people in order to obtain money.

Hale tried to recruit other criminals to kill William Smith and his wife when Spencer rejected him, but they all turned him down.

Following the Smith massacre, Hale started to worry that "Ace" Kirby would reveal Hale's involvement in the killings.

He so convinced Kirby to try robbing a grocery shop, where he would supposedly discover priceless jewels.

The business owner was then notified of the precise hour of the planned heist.

When Kirby broke through a window to enter the store, he was met by multiple shotgun bursts, which ultimately proved fatal.

Thus, Hale and his friends were spared the testimony of a second witness.

Ernest Burkhart was the first to own up to his role as the weak point in the Hale organization.

Burkhart was a weak-willed person who was totally controlled by Hale and would comply with his uncle's wishes without hesitation.

John Ramsey also came clean about his involvement in the killings after discovering the extent of the evidence the FBI agents had gathered.

In an effort to get Ernest Burkhart to retract his testimony, Hale and his accomplices tried to subdue him once more.

Ernest personally begged for protection from the FBI, fearing that Hale would have him assassinated.

Ernest Burkhart was put on the witness stand at Hale's preliminary hearing.

Hale's lawyer said that they were Burkhart's representative and asked to speak with him for a little while before he testified.

This request was approved, and while the layers were speaking with Ernest, the court adjourned.

He was then brought to Fairfax, Oklahoma, where he was consulted by a number of Hales's friends and family members who pleaded with him to follow their legal advice.

Agents not only solved the crimes but also found that Ernest's full-blood Osage wife, Mollie Burkhart, was slowly poisoning herself to death.

It is a well-established truth that her health returned right away when she was freed from Burkhart and Hale's influence.

Ernest, Hale's nephew, would have inherited the Lizzie Q family's whole fortune upon Mollie's passing.

Two Federal District Court trials in Guthrie, Oklahoma; one Federal District Court trial in Oklahoma City, Oklahoma; and one Federal District Court trial in Pawhuska, Oklahoma were held for William K. Hale and John Ramsey.

For the murder of Henry Roan, they were found guilty and given a life term at the Federal Penitentiary in Leavenworth, Kansas.

The sole area under US control was the site of Henry Roan's murder.

For homicides over which the US lacked jurisdiction, state courts handed down other penalties.

For his involvement in the killing of William E. Smith and his family, Ernest Burkhart was sentenced to life in prison.

After killing Anna Brown, Kelsey Morrison was sentenced to life in prison.

Bryan Burkhart was never found guilty despite turning state evidence in state court.

The Federal District Court's decision in the first trial of Hale and Ramsey that it lacked jurisdiction was overturned in a relatively short amount of time—just twenty-five days—by the US Supreme Court.

A hung jury was the outcome of Hale and Ramsey's second trial in the Federal Court at Guthrie.

After the Federal District Court in Oklahoma City dismissed the case, Hale and Ramey were found guilty and sentenced to life in prison.

Due to an error in district of trial, Hale's conviction was overturned upon filing an appeal. Ramsey's conviction was automatically overturned by this ruling as well.

In the Federal District Court in Pawhuska, Oklahoma, Hale and Ramsey requested a severance during their most recent trial.

As a consequence, they were found guilty and given life sentences.Hale's attorneys used every tactic—both legal and illicit—to win their client's release.

6

Chapter

The Trials

The Department of Justice knew exactly how powerful Hale was and that it would be very hard to punish him in a state court.

So they looked into the different killings to see if any of them may serve as the foundation for a federal prosecution as opposed to a state prosecution.

Federal jurisdiction originated from crimes committed on Indian land.

However, only state courts may hear cases involving crimes committed on territory that was sold to white people or that was not otherwise governed by a tribe.

Since Roan was killed on an Osage allotment, this case appeared to have the most potential for federal jurisdiction.

Charges were filed in Oklahoma federal district court against Hale and Ramsey for the murder of Henry Roan.

John Leahy, an attorney employed by the Osage Tribal Council, and U.S. Attorney Roy St. Lewis were members of the prosecution team. Leahy was thereafter referred to by Tom White as a man of "splendid character" and "one of the best attorneys in the state of Oklahoma."

Early in January 1926, grand jury hearings got underway.

The New York Times stated: *"Seldom in the long history of the white man's dubious dealings with the Indian has there been such a determined combination of craft and violence as that described by witnesses before the grand jury."*

The grand jury was persuaded by the evidence to return the desired indictments.

Jim Springer, the local lawyer Hale selected to defend John Ramsey and who had a reputation for moving quickly, didn't take long to persuade his client to retract his confession.

"I have never killed anyone," Ramsey said at this point.

Springer will attempt every ruse known to man, starting with the grand jury trials in January 1926.

In order to diminish the credibility of their evidence, he and his colleagues coerced witnesses into lying, threatened potentially hostile witnesses, bought off jurors, and made ludicrous statements that were unfounded.

For instance, Springer said that Burkhart and Ramsey's signatures were obtained only after they had been tortured by government investigators.

(The strategies would so enrage White and J. Edgar Hoover that they would put pressure on the Department of Justice to bring charges against both Springer and the perjury defense witnesses.)

"Hale's lawyers employed every device, legal and illegal, to obtain their client's freedom," according to an FBI report of the case.

Ernest Burkhart was, in Hale's opinion, the greatest threat. Burkhart was right to worry for his life.

Burkhart informed White on January 20 that he thought he would soon be *"bumped off,"* and White made arrangements for Burkhart to be taken out of state and placed under protection until his trial.

He used a pseudonym while registering at hotels.

While *"every precaution is being taken,"* White expressed concern in a letter to Hoover that someone employed by Hale would "slip poison" Burkhart.

Prosecutors received unfavorable news on March 1.

The trial judge decided that the murder case would have to go forward, if at all, in state court since an Osage allotment is not the same as tribal property.

The federal government promptly declared that it will file an appeal with the US Supreme Court over the ruling.

They did, however, arrange for the men to be arrested on state murder charges in order to stop Hale and Ramsey from evading any legal action.

It would be very hard to get a jury in Osage County to convict, but they were out of options.

Pawhuska's preliminary hearing on March 12 was quite the show.

The Tulsa Tribune stated that *"such a crowd has seldom, if ever, been gathered in a courtroom before."*

An audience that included *"society women"* and *"well-groomed businessmen"* was joined by *"cowboys in broad-brimmed hats"* and *"Osage chiefs in beaded garb."*

It was Mollie Burkhart.
Hale's spouse was also in agreement. Up until Ernest Burkhart entered the stand in the afternoon session, everything proceeded very normally.

On the grounds that Burkhart had not been informed of his rights, one of Hale's attorneys stood up and requested permission to speak with him in private.

"This gentleman is my client," he said.

When the court asked Burkhart if the lawyer's claim was accurate, he said, *"He's not my attorney, but I'm willing to talk to him."*

Burkhart left the witness stand and hurried to the judge's chambers to speak with Hale's attorneys, much to the dismay of the prosecution.

Half an hour later, Sargent Freeling, Hale's lawyer, came out of the room to request that Burkhart be allowed to meet with the defense team for the remainder of the day.

The magistrate concurred.

Burkhart took the stand once more the following morning in court, this time as a witness for the defense rather than the prosecution.

Burkhart testified that he never spoke with Hale about Roan's murder, reversing his January account.

Hale smiled, watching as Burkhart took back sentence after sentence.

Trial of Ernest Burkhart

Ernest Burkhart's trial for his part in the Smith home bombing got underway in May.

Burkhart was tried in Pawhuska state court exclusively for Bill Smith's murder.

Ernest's attorneys at Hale were keen to get him acquitted because they understood that if he was found guilty, he would probably testify against the government in the Roan case.

To demonstrate that Ramsey and Burkhart's admissions were forced, the defense presented testimony.

All of it was untrue, but it didn't matter. It was dramatic stuff.

According to Hale's testimony, as he turned to see that a federal agent had cocked a weapon behind his head, Agent *"Smith jumped across the room, grabbed me by the shoulder, and shoved a big gun in my face."*

Tom White allegedly said to him, *"We will have you put in the hot chair."*

He said that after that, agents had forced him into a chair, covered his head with a black hood, and fastened to it a device that resembled a catcher's mask.

"They talked about putting the juice on me." *"Don't you smell that human flesh burning?"* yelled one agent after taking a whiff.

Such testimony draws interest.

Articles concerning the purportedly terrible treatment of a prisoner by federal officials appeared in The Washington Post and other major media.

Tom White responded to J. Edgar Hoover's demand for an explanation by labeling Hale's account as a *"fabrication from start to finish."*

Prosecutors and defense lawyers yelled at one another in the courtroom, and one prosecutor threatened to meet a defense lawyer *"out in the courtyard."*

The Court disregarded the evidence. Burkhart's January confession in Guthrie was not predicated on the account of torture provided by Hale and Ramsey.

The court stated that he did not believe the claims made by Hale and Ramsey to be credible.

Burkhart's statement was excluded, the judge said, because it was made early in the morning following a lengthy period of incarceration.

However, Kelsie Morrison was a crucial player for the prosecution in the Burkhart case.

Morrison had admitted to his part in Anna Brown's death on May 18 in Guthrie.

Morrison said that after driving Anna to a location approximately three miles from Fairfax, he and Byran Burkhart had her intoxicated.

Following what he described as *"about forty steps"* into a ravine, he *"gave her a big drink and left her."*

After two or three hours, he used a rifle that Hale had given him to shoot Anna.

Anna "fell back down" silently. He said Hale paid him $1600 for the work.

Morrison had a lot to say about the Smith house explosion as well.

He said that he had been contacted *"any number of times"* by Hale to shoot Bill Smith and his wife *"at his home at night,"* but he had declined.

According to him, Mollie would get the properties if the Smiths were killed, *"and then Ernest Burkhart would make it right with me."*

The Ernest Burkhart family's inheritance could have increased by around $150,000 as a result of the triple murders.

Tom White, who was present at the trial, reported that Burkhart *"seemed to be very restless and nervous"* the whole time.

On June 8, Ernest Burkhart handed a note to a deputy sheriff who was transporting him back to jail from the courthouse after his trial had been halted by the unexpected death of his and Mollies' four-year-old daughter.

Burkhart wanted to meet with prosecutor John Leahy, according to the message.

In his cell, Burkhart told the two men he was "through lying" and that he didn't "want to go on with this trial any longer."

Hale may have murdered him, so he was unable to inform his own attorney.

Upon Burkhart's subsequent court appearance, he approached the judge directly, exchanged a few words with him, and then said in front of the astonished defense team and the crowded courtroom, *"I want to dismiss the defense attorneys."*

"I now have Mr. [Flint] Moss representing me." Moss said, *"Mr. Burkhart wishes to*

withdraw his plea of not guilty and enter a plea of guilty."

Burkhart read from a statement that he had brought Asa Kirby, Hale's soup man, the news that the time had come to blow up the Smith residence.

"I feel in my heart that I did it because I was requested to do it by Hale, who is my uncle."
Burkhart further acknowledged that the claim that federal officers had physically abused her was untrue.

He stated the only stress was having to answer questions for extended periods of time at night. Burkhart received a life sentence on June 21, 1926.

Hale-Ramsey Trial

By May, the U.S. Supreme Court had decided that federal court may hold the Hale-Ramsey trial for Henry Roan's murder.

The trial began on July 26, 1926, in the Guthrie brick courtroom with prosecution witnesses well guarded.

The prosecution inquired of each prospective juror during voir dire whether they had been contacted by anybody seeking a certain verdict since they were aware that it would be difficult to find twelve untainted jurors.

They all vowed not to have. However, the prosecutors were worried about more.

According to one Osage, many white Oklahomans saw the death of a Native American as a crime comparable to "cruelty to animals." The victim was a Native American.

The main witness for the prosecution was Ernest Burkhart.

With tears in his eyes, he had admitted responsibility and promised White that he would always speak the truth in court going forward, no matter what the repercussions.

Burkhart informed the jury that Hale had originally intended to use poisoned moonshine—a tactic he had successfully used in the past—to murder Roan.

(During the *"reign of terror,"* more osage were poisoned than could be killed by other means.)

According to his testimony, Hale lost his cool when he realized Ramsey had shot Roan in the back of the head and grabbed the pistol.

In order to give the impression that Roan committed suicide, Ramsey was supposed to have shot him in the front of the head and then left the gun by his side.

Had he merely done as instructed, Hale had said that *"nobody would have known."*

According to bootlegger Matt Williams' testimony, in January 1923, Hale told him that he had taken out a $25,000 life insurance policy with Denver Insurance company on Henry Roan.

Since Hale had given Roan a few animals as a loan, he could pretend that the policy was "security for the cattle deal."

He went on, saying he had arranged for John Ramsey to "bump Roan off."

Williams testified that he met with John Ramsey three days after Roan's death, and Ramsey informed him that he had shot Roan after enticing him with alcohol.

It's interesting to note that Williams claimed Hale had previously considered his legal approach.

He informed Williams that he had discussed with his attorneys the possibility of federal charges for *"pulling off jobs"* on Indian territory, and that attorney had given him the assurance that *"the government had no jurisdiction."*

In his testimony, Dick Gregg, a bank robber from the infamous Al Spencer gang, said that Hale had made an unsuccessful attempt to recruit him to kill Osage members.

O. C. Webb stated in court that he overheard Hale say to Ramsey, *"We are ready to go—everything is ready to go,"* prior to the Roan murder.

Additional witness evidence centered on Hale's policy about Roan's life.

According to an insurance examiner's testimony, Hale said, *"Oh God, I am—hell yes!"* when he was asked if he was going to murder "that Indian" for his insurance.

Hale testified for the defense, saying, *"I never came up with a plan to have Roan assassinated. I never wanted him to go."*

In addition, the defense produced other witnesses to testify who either supported Hale or Ramsey's alibis or attempted to place the blame on an outlaw named Curley Johnson, who has since passed away, or Roy Bunch, who had been having an affair with Roan's wife.

A large portion of the testimony was falsified and was purchased by Hale.

Typical was the evidence of Buster Jarrett, who at the time of the trial was being held in a Pawhuska jail on a charge of bank robbery and claimed that he had witnessed Roy Bunch pay Curley Johnson to kill Roan.

(Jarrett later admitted that Hale's lawyer had convinced him to provide his fabricated evidence during a ninety-minute visit to his detention cell. Assuming Hale testified as requested, his lawyer threatened to "snatch him out of prison".)

Prosecutor Roy St. Lewis informed the jury during his final statement that the evidence demonstrated how *"the richest tribe of Indians on the globe has become the illegitimate prey of white men."* And the defendant, *"the ruthless freebooter of death,"* has shown to be the worst predator of them all.

After five days of deliberation, the jury was unable to reach a decision.

In court, St. Lewis revealed that he was aware of the cause: at least one juror, if not more, had been bought off.

(It was later discovered that the jury divided 6 to 6 on the guilt verdict.) Another trial was to take place.

On October 20, the retrial got underway in Oklahoma City.

The retrial's witness list for the prosecution was the same as it was in the first trial, but the witness questioning was more focused and condensed.

The defense attempted to hold Ernest Burkhart accountable for the killing of Roan.

Burkhart said that he had entered a guilty plea for the murders of his wife's spouse, sister, and domestic helper.

With a litany of killed and likely murdered Mollie's relatives in hand, Hale's lawyer posed the question, *"Has your wife no any surviving relatives outside of the two children she has by you?"*

"She has not," in response from Burkhart.

Following a full day of consideration, the jury declared their decision.

Ramsey and Hale were taken aback when the clerk announced the decision.

Found guilty—found guilty of first-degree murder.

On the first ballot, there had been a unanimous vote.

Prison was imposed on the two men for the "period of your natural lives." To carry out their terms, Hale and Ramsey were sent to Leavenworth, Kansas.

The two men would meet Tom White, the recently appointed warden, a few months later.

Kelsie Morrison was put on trial in 1927 for the murder of Anna Brown.

Morrison had denied making the confession, and after Hale's letter to him was intercepted by prison officials, it was revealed that he had even threatened to *"burn"* down the government *"if I ever get the chance."*

In the event that Morrison was summoned as a witness in Hale's trial, he assured his "old friend" that *"I won't forget you"* and *"I will be there with bells on."*

Bryan Burkhart, who possessed immunity and provided testimony for the prosecution, was cleared in his own state court trial for the murder of Anna Brown.

Katherine Cole, Morrison's ex-wife, also did.

Cole stated in her testimony that she witnessed Bryan Burkhart and Morrison leading an inebriated Anna Brown from their automobile to a ravine.

"I was terrified when I discovered that they were planning to harm Anna Brown. I was scared that Kelsie might hurt me, so I didn't want to talk to him." She testified that they came back, but Anna was gone, around thirty minutes later.

When she questioned Kelsie about what had transpired later that evening, Kelsie *"cursed me and told me to keep my mouth shut."*
Katherine Cole had valid concerns.

Kelsie instructed him to *"get rid of Katherine"*— that is, kill her—because *"she knew too much about the Anna Brown murder deal,"* according to testimony from another witness, Dewey Selph.

Hale and Selph later met to talk about Selph's unfulfilled plans to kill Cole.
Bootlegger Matt Williams said in court that he saw Burkhart the evening of Brown's murder.
Kelsie Morrison was going to meet them at the Arkansas River Bridge, Burkhart informed

him, adding that *"he had to take care of some business for Uncle Bill that night"*.

Williams said that he encountered Morrison three or four days later, who informed him that Hale had *"him do the worst job he ever pulled"* and that Hale was now refusing to give him the money he had promised for murdering Anna.

Williams stated that Morrison hit Anna from behind *"while Bryan Burkhart was loving Anna"* before carrying her out of the car and shooting her in the head.

Morrison was found guilty by the jury.

Hale-Ramsey Final Trials

But the ordeal was not yet over.

Hale and Ramsey filed an appeal of their verdicts.

The Eighth Circuit came to the conclusion that the trial was held in the incorrect court.

Instead of being prosecuted in the northern district of Oklahoma, where the crime is purported to have taken place, Hale and Ramsey were tried in federal court for the western district of Oklahoma.

Hale and Ramsey requested the termination of their trials. They each had a separate trial.

Ramsey was found guilty 10 months after Hale's January 1929 conviction.

Repercussions

The trials had come to an end.

Most of the time, the killings ceased. However, this did not imply that all killers had been apprehended.

In the book "Killers of the Flower Moon: The Osage Murders and the Birth of the FBI" by the bestselling Author "David Grann", observes that the 1920s murder spree continues to haunt Osage generations to this day.

The killings are still *"in the back of our minds...you just have it in the back of your head that you don't trust anybody,"* according to Henry Roan's great-grandson.

Grann writes about his attempts to identify some of the murderers who got away with it in a whole chapter of his book.

The bestselling author identified Herbert G. Burt, a bank president and close friend of Hale, as one of the possible murderers.
Burt became extremely wealthy by making loans to the Osage "at astronomical interest rates."

It was said that Burt was motivated by money and was responsible for the death of lawyer W. W. Vaughan, who was thrown from a speeding train after meeting with George Bigheart.

The evidence of Charles Whitehorm murder case pointed to three persons as the murderers:

Whitehorn's half-Cheyenne, half-white wife Hattie Whitehorn, and two further accomplices.

Although the FBI had first considered the Whitehorn case, it had abandoned it because the evidence *"did not fit into the bureau's dramatic theory of the murders: that a lone mastermind (Hale) was responsible for all the killings."*

From the Whitehorn case, a crucial lesson was learnt: *"The evil of Hale was not an anomaly."*

It was observed that, in contrast to the official estimate of twenty-four killings by the FBI, researchers and academics ``*now believe that the Osage death toll was in the scores, if not the hundreds."*

It's possible that the majority of the victims perished from difficult-to-identify poisons, such as morphine injections given to Osage members who were already intoxicated.

In nearly all of these situations, the fatalities that ensued would be classified as alcohol poisoning deaths.

Among the list of murders and the "web of silent conspirators" who support them were several of Osage County's most influential white people.

Bankers, physicians, dealers, undertakers, attorneys, affluent ranchers, and even law enforcement officials are on the list.

And the principal actors in the drama unfolding at the bureau? Mollie separated from Ernest Burkhart amid the federal trials.

In 1928, she wed again. An earlier decision pronouncing Mollie incapable was canceled in 1931 by a court, allowing her to spend her money as she pleased.

Mollie passed away at the age of 50 in 1937.

In 1947, John Ramsey received parole. After being granted parole in 1937, Ernest Burkhart stole a bank before being allowed to go again in 1959.

He lived out his latter years with his brother Bryan in a trailer.

William Hale was granted release in 1947 after serving 21 years in Leavenworth.

He worked on a pig farm for a large portion of his incarceration.

Tom White, the warden of Leavenworth, insisted on treating Hale like any other prisoner at all times.

Hale never acknowledged giving the order to kill. Hale penned a letter expressing his wish to return to Osage County before he was released from jail.

"I had rather live at Gray Horse than any place on earth." It was not to be, though.

He had to remain outside the state of Oklahoma as a requirement of his parole.

Hale was buried in Wichita, Kansas, after passing away at a nursing facility in Arizona in 1962.

More over 10,000 people are currently part of the Osage Nation, however fewer of them reside in Osage County.

The 1920s boomtowns are essentially extinct. The "stripper" wells, which typically yield less than 15 gallons per day, have mostly replaced the gushing oil wells of the past.

Approximately 75% of the oil headrights on the Osage tribe are still held by members.

The Osage now appears prepared to switch from oil to a more environmentally friendly energy source.

A brand-new windmill farm emerged in Osage County in 2015. It's a changing time.

Nowadays, money from casinos exceeds that from oil. In 2016, the Osage fortune made it possible for the Tribe to buy media magnate Ted Turner's 43,000-acre Bluestem estate.

The oldest tribally owned museum in the United States, the Osage Nation Museum in Pawhuska, Oklahoma, offers exhibitions on Osage art, culture, and history, including the Reign of Terror.

7

Chapter

Statements and confessions

STATEMENT OF FRED WHEELER, Ralston, Okla.

Q. Did you spend May 21, 1923, in Ralston? A. Certainly, sir.

Q. On this particular day, did you see Bryan Burkhart and Anna Brown? A. Certainly, sir.

Q. Describe what you witnessed that day in your own words.

As Ben Jones asked Joe McGuire if the person in the car was Anna Brown, Joe McGuire turned to face me and said, *"Shorty, wasn't that Anna Brow in that car?"*

I replied, *"Yes, it was."*

Two people, Anna Brown and Bryan Burkhart, had driven up in a car and asked about getting something to eat.

Just as they were leaving, Joe McGuire asked Ben Jones if the person in the car was Anna Brown.

Ben Jones said, *"I'm going down and to shake hands with her; I haven't seen her in a long time,"* as they continued down the street and came to a stop in front of Bob McSpadden's restaurant.

After a minute, both Ben Jones and Joe McGuire stood there, and I walked down the street, stopped, and took a seat about thirty feet away from the car.

When they drove away, Joe McGuire followed suit and got within twenty feet of the vehicle, at which point Anna Brown turned around and yelled something at Joe McGuire.

Bryan Jones had begun in that direction and was roughly in the middle of the block when they departed.

They proceeded straight west through the town, and I'm not sure where they went after that.

Ernest Burkhart's statements (January 6, 1926)

The first is Ernest Burkhart's statement about Henry Roan's murder.

I went to Henry Grammer's ranch with Bill Hale a few weeks before Henry Roan was discovered dead.

Bill Hale pointed me toward a man who was working for Grammer and identified him as John Ramsey, telling me he was a man who would stand pat and keep his mouth shut.

That was when Henry Grammer was once found in possession of some stolen cattle, Grammer persuaded Ramsey to confess to stealing the animals, clearing Grammer of any wrongdoing.

Ramsey thereafter spent a sentence in McAlester Penitentiary for the theft of these livestock.

Hale obtained a $25,000 life insurance policy on Henry Roan approximately a year and a half prior to Roan's death.

He informed me that the reason he obtained the policy was because Henry Roan had family issues, was a heavy drinker, had attempted suicide once, and Hale did not think he would live long.

When Hale and I left Grammer's property and he showed me where Ramsey was, Hale threatened to track out Henry Roan and predicted that Ramsey would either shoot him and leave a gun next to him, leading everyone to believe he had committed suicide.

A few days later, Ramsey visited Fairfax, and as I was passing by, I overheard Ramsey and Bill Hale chatting about purchasing a Ford Roadster in Ponca City.

After that, Ramsey departed, saying he would travel to Ponca via Pawnee and Perry rather than Santa Fe and Frisco.

After Ramsey departed, Hale informed me that he had given Ramsey the money to purchase a Ford Roadster because Ramsey would need to guide Roan about, follow him, and bring him to a location where he could bump him since Ramsey had no means to murder Roan and escape.

Within a few days, Ramsey came back to Fairfax driving a brand-new Ford Roadster that, from what I gather, he purchased in Ponca City.

For a few days afterward, I noticed Ramsey driving this automobile about town.

Ramsey approached me on the street at Fairfax, about a week before Henry Roan's death was discovered, and asked to speak with Hale.

I informed him that I had no idea where he was. I visited Hale later and informed him what Ramsey had said.

Ramsey then urged me to tell Hale the work was all fine and not to worry, that it had happened out in the Sol Smith paddock.

Ramsey departed Fairfax and headed to his Ripley residence. After returning to Fairfax a few days earlier, Ramsey went to Grammer's house.

Henry Roan's corpse was discovered dead in his automobile not long after. A few days later, Ramsey returned to Fairfax, had a brief visit, and then continued on to Ripley.

Bill Hale told me he had given Ramsey the remaining sum he owed for killing Roan sometime after Roan's body was discovered, maybe a month later.

This meant the job cost him $1,000 in total—the Ford automobile plus the outstanding amount.

I asked Ramsey about the incident a while after Roan's body was discovered.

Ramsey replied that he had met Roan on the route that ran from Fairfax to Burbank.

He then got into Roan's car, sat on the back seat, and they drove off, under the hill, with him promising to get them a drink.

When they arrived at the proper location, out of sight of the road, he shot Roan, walked back to the top of the hill, where he had left his car, and continued into Fairfax.

He informed me that he used a.45 automatic handgun to shoot Roan.

Ernest Burkhart's Declaration About the Murders of Rita and Bill Smith.

Made the following declaration on January 6, 1926, in Guthrie, Oklahoma, to Agents M. S. Smith, John K. Wren, and T. B. White.

Bill Hale and W. E. Smith exchanged money at some point in 1918, with Hale lending Smith $5,500.00.

I recall that sometime in 1920, or maybe even 1919, Hale informed me that he had received a check for $6,000.00 from W. E. Smith.

Of that sum, $5,500.00 would settle Smith's debt to Hale, and the remaining $500.00 would cover interest.

Later, while I was visiting Bill Hale's ranch, W. E. Smith and his wife drove up, and I overheard them conversing.

I was a hundred yards or so away near the barn. Smith and his spouse quickly fled.

Following their departure, Hale approached the barn and informed me that Smith had requested that he return the $6,000.00 check that he had previously given to Hale.

Smith was attempting to convey to his spouse that Hale owed Smith $6,000.00. Shortly afterward, Smith drove up on his own once more.

Smith departed again after Hale went to where he was and they conversed for around twenty minutes.

Hale informed me a while after Smith departed that he would not return the money to Smith because he had waited too long for Smith to reimburse him.

There was animosity between Hale and Smith ever since.

Hale informed me that he thought he might have bumped off Smith at some point, maybe a year or more later.

Subsequently, Hale informed me that he thought he would have Smith fired.

Hale later confided in me that he had either gone to visit Al Spencer or had planned to meet Al Spencer in order to get him to scold Smith.

As far as I can recall, this chat took place around a year before Smith's death.

Hale told me something about not knowing where Spencer was and about persuading Fred Rowe to accompany him to visit Spencer around this time.

I can't recall what exactly occurred to Spencer.

Afterwards, Hale informed me that he was heading to visit Grammer and ask him to provide a guy to push Smith, and he really went—or at least stated he was heading to Grammer's.

A week or two later, Hale informed me that Grammer had advised him to trust Blackie Thompson more than anybody else and that Blackie would do the task.

Hale said he would go visit Al Spencer.

He stated he didn't know where Spencer was, but he would ask Max Billingsley to go with him and bring him information.

After a span of two or three weeks, he claimed to have spoken with Al Spencer, who was now abroad.

Hale then indicated that he would see Grammer, and shortly afterward, he said that Grammer had informed him that Blackie Thompson would do the task.

Hale informed me later that Blackie was either missing or had left the country.

Statements from Witnesses in the Hale-Ramsey Trial for Henry Roan's Murder

Fairfax; Harry Corbett. Okla signed a statement stating that defendant Hale had purchased him a new Ford automobile in order to do a task for him, as John Ramsey had informed him before Henry Roan was killed. In January 1923, Ramsey made frequent visits to Corbett's house in a brand-new Ford automobile.

MATT M. WILLIAMS of Pawruska, Oklahoma, stated that Hale had "propositioned" him to "bump" Henry Roan out, and that he had subsequently informed him that John Ramsey had been hired to complete the task.Will attest that W.K. Hale informed him he had a $25,000 life insurance policy on Henry Roan not long before the latter was discovered dead.

Before murdering Roan, O.C. WEBB of Fairfax, Oklahoma, signed a statement claiming to have overheard a discussion between W.K. Hale and John Ramsey, during which John Ramsey informed Hale, *"We are ready to go."* *"Everything is prepared for departure,"* and W.K. Hale added, *"Be certain and don't falter."* The night before Webb was arrested, W.K. Hale assured him that he would rely on him to "stand pat."

Charles Doty of Webb City, Oklahoma, signed a statement referring to a statement made by Whitie White of Webb City regarding a defense counsel offering him $500 in exchange for delivering a false testimony at the case's initial trial.

Witness: Bob Parker, Fairfax, Oklahoma. Will attest that he knew Henry Roan well; that on or around February 6, 1923, George Pratt informed him about the discovery of an automobile in Sel Smith's pasture; that he and Fairfax resident Jim Rhodes went to the car, where Henry Roan's lifeless body was discovered, and that an inspection was conducted of the vehicle and body.

W. C. SPURGEON, Fairfax, Oklahoma, Witness. Attested that, as a member of the coroner's jury, he inspected Henry Roan's body when it was discovered on February 6, 1923, and that he was intimately acquainted with the man throughout his existence. Regarding the body's posture and the wounds, Mr. Spurgeon is qualified to testify.

J. S. SHOON, MD, Fairfax, Ok. attested that he examined the corpse and wounds and that he was a close personal friend of Henry Roan throughout his live.

Mr. White also testified about an encounter he had with Hale at the Federal Penitentiary in Leavenworth, Kansas, where he has served as warden.

During Hale's current detention there, Mr. White was informed by Hale that he had always expressed regret for the falsehoods he had made on the witness stand about how he and other government agents had subjected him to an electric cap and other harsh measures, and that Hale had also promised to make amends to Mr. White when he told his wife and lawyer about the lies he had told.

JOHN McCLAIN, Tulsa, Oklahoma; Witness and Agent, Mutual Life Insurance Co. attested that in 1921, he met W. K. Hale in Pawhuska, Oklahoma, and asked him for the names of Indians for whom he could write a life insurance policy.

He told Hale that he had been speaking with Henry Roan, but that he was unaware that Roan could obtain a policy.

Hale then asked, *"What Henry Roan?" "I will take that bet, pay the premium, and make it payable to me,"* Hale said at that point.

Regarding Henry Roan's life, an application was submitted, but it was turned down.

DR. W. H. Aaron, Pawhuska, Oklahoma, Witness, testified that he examined Henry Roan for the Mutual Life Insurance Company of New York, of which John McClain was an agent in 1921, and that he also represented the Capital Life Insurance Company of Denver in relation to a $25,000 policy payable to W. K. Hale.

Dr. Aaron also testified that while Bill Hale was present during Henry Roan's examination, he was asked whether he was going to kill the Indian for his insurance and who would benefit from it. Hale said, *"Oh God, I am—hell, yes!"*

Witness: Ernest Burghart; Oklahoma State Prison; McAlaster, Oklahoma. Nephew of Defendant Hale, who testified that he and W.K. Hale met John Ramsey in the fall of 1922 at the home of the late Henry Grammer, and that during their alone conversation, Hale informed Burkhart that he had a life insurance policy on the life of Henry Raon and that he could rely on John Ramsey to "bump" Henry Roan off.

Additionally, Burkhart also testified about an exchange with Hale during which Hale said he would accompany John Ramsey to Pawnee, Oklahoma, to pick up a car, and that he would pay Ramsey $500 to purchase the vehicle.

Burkhart testified also regarding an exchange that occurred between him and John Ramsey regarding the latter's purchase of a car in Ponca City, Oklahoma, a few days later; additionally, he testified regarding an exchange that occurred between the two in Fairfax, Oklahoma, approximately thirty minutes after Henry Roan's death.

In that exchange, Ramsey asked Burkhart where Bill Hale was, stating that he (Ramsey) wanted to see Hale that night; Ramsey further requested that Burkhart see Hale to inform him that the job was completed and that he had "bumped" that Indian in a canyon in Sol Smith's pasture.

Finally, Burkhart testified regarding an exchange that occurred between Ramsey and Ramsey at Fairfax, Oklahoma.

Furthermore, Ernest Burkhart added that his brother Horace Burkhart had informed him that shortly before Henry Roan was assassinated, he (Bosarth) had observed Bill Hale and John Ramsey playing pool in either McElroy's or Evans' pool hall at Fairfax; that Hale had given a cue, telling Ramsey to meet him somewhere (though Horace was unsure of the location); that Bosarth and Hale left the pool hall through the front door, while Ramsey left through the back door.

Hale and Ramsey met a short distance away, at which point Hale pulled aside and gave him some cash.

Made in United States
Troutdale, OR
05/06/2024

19684575R00086